ANCIENT ROME

First published in the UK in 2019 by

Ivy Kids

An imprint of The Quarto Group
The Old Brewery
6 Blundell Street
London N7 9BH
United Kingdom
www.QuartoKnows.com

British Library Cataloguing-in-Publication Data
A catalogue record for this book is available from the British Library.

ISBN: 978-1-78240-900-7

This book was conceived, designed & produced by

Ivy Kids

58 West Street, Brighton BN1 2RA, United Kingdom

PUBLISHER Susan Kelly
MANAGING EDITOR Susie Behar
ART DIRECTOR Hanri van Wyk
DESIGNER Kevin Knight
IN-HOUSE DESIGNER Kate Haynes
IN-HOUSE EDITORS Lucy Menzies &
Hannah Dove
BLACK AND WHITE ILLUSTRATIONS BY Jack Xander

Manufactured in Guangdong, China TT052019

1 3 5 7 9 10 8 6 4 2

My FIRST
Fact File

ANCIENT ROME

EVERYTHING you NEED to KNOW

BY SIMON HOLLAND   ILLUSTRATED BY ADAM HILL
CONSULTANT: DR MATTHEW NICHOLLS

IVY KIDS

CONTENTS

EVERYTHING you NEED to KNOW

INTRODUCTION

We hear about them all the time, but who were the ancient Romans and why do we still talk about them? The Romans are famous for many things: their great engineers and inventors, their powerful politicians, big thinkers and awesome armies, their incredible artists and craftspeople, and their mysterious gods and goddesses.

How did they get to be so great? Well, they were brilliant at borrowing ideas from other people and adding them to their own ideas and ways of life. They helped themselves to the best things they could find! Then, with the help of their armies, they took over many other lands, built an empire and spread their ways of life far and wide.

So, even though the history of the Romans began more than 3,000 years ago, we still see lots of Roman ideas all around us. Every time you turn on a tap or check your calendar, you are using a Roman invention. Each time you travel along a long road or cross an arched bridge, you are using something that was developed in Roman times. Every time you see a show, go to a party or a leisure centre, you are doing something the Romans also enjoyed. You're a lot more Roman than you think you are!

In this book, you will see the terms 'CE' and 'BCE'. 'CE' means 'Common Era', or during the age of Christianity. 'BCE' means 'Before the Common Era', or before Christianity.

The ancient Romans are known for the long, straight roads they built across their Empire.

HOW ROME BEGAN

Rome began as a group of small farming villages. There were many hills in this area of Italy. On two of the hills, the Palatine Hill and Capitoline Hill, there were settlements. These settlements eventually grew to become a central part of Rome. There were other villages in the area, too, so they may all have come together to form a small kingdom, possibly from around 625 BCE. There was also a river, the River Tiber, which was very important since it meant that food and other goods could be shipped from the coast to the new villages.

QUICK FACTS

A group of people called the Etruscans arrived in the area in around 650 BCE. They came from the eastern Mediterranean and they built towns and cities. Some of Rome's first kings were Etruscan.

ROMULUS AND REMUS

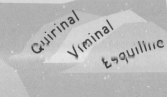

Rome was built on several hills, with the Palatine and Capitoline hills at the centre.

Capitoline
Quirinal
Viminal
Esquilline
River Tiber
Palatine
Caelian
Aventine

Romans believed that the city of Rome was created by the sons of a god. Romulus and Remus were twin sons of Mars, the god of war. As babies, they were left in a basket on the River Tiber. When the basket ran aground, the twins were discovered by a she-wolf that, along with a woodpecker, fed them, before a shepherd found the twins and took them in. When they grew up, the brothers decided to build a city, but disagreed over where to build it. Romulus killed Remus and named his city — Rome — after himself.

The first Romans were farmers and shepherds.

THE REPUBLIC

Rome was originally ruled by a king elected by the people. The first six kings built temples and city walls, set up chariot races and boxing competitions for the public to enjoy, and expanded the kingdom by conquering nearby lands. But the seventh king, Tarquin the Proud, used force to control the people. In 509 BCE, Tarquin was overthrown and the Romans began to make their land into a 'republic'. Power was now held by the people. The people chose officials to run the state and make decisions. These officials were called magistrates, and they were advised by a small number of aristocrats from rich, powerful families, who made up the Senate.

QUICK FACTS

The Senate controlled state spending, Rome's rule of its Empire and advised the magistrates.

THE SENATE

The members of the Senate weren't elected by the people. They were chosen by important Romans. Their role was to discuss the political issues of the state and give out written decrees — or official advice — for the magistrates and consuls to follow when waging wars or spending public money. The Senate was often a rowdy place, full of speeches interrupted by shouts, boos and arguments about how money was to be spent!

Elected magistrates shared power and represented the people of Rome.

Senators held regular meetings in the 'Curia' (Senate House).

Many senators were famous for their persuasive public speaking, called 'oratory'.

The two consuls were the highest-ranking members of the government.

THE EMPIRE AND ITS EMPERORS

By the 1st century BCE, Rome had taken over most of Italy, and had even more land from neighbouring countries. However the top-ranking Romans began to fight amongst themselves. After defeating his rivals, one man, Octavian, became Rome's first emperor. He took the name Caesar Augustus in 27 BCE. From then, until the end of the Empire in 1453, 250 men served as emperors. Some were good and some were bad. With power firmly in their hands, they were able to act in any way they chose.

Caesar Augustus (27 BCE – 14 CE)

The first Roman emperor, who used his strong army to bring peace and stability.

Caligula (37 – 41 CE)

He ignored the Senate, spent lavishly and insisted he was a god.

Nero (54 – 68 CE)

A brutal leader, he had his enemies executed, including his own wife!

Trajan (98 – 117 CE)

The Empire reached its greatest extent under Trajan, the 'great conqueror'.

GAUL
(MODERN-DAY FRANCE)

ITALY

MEDITERRANEAN

The Roman Empire was at its greatest in around 117 CE.

Diocletian
(284–305 CE)

He divided the Empire into four regions. Each region had a separate ruler.

Constantine
(306–337 CE)

The first Christian emperor, he moved his capital to Byzantium (modern-day Turkey).

BE AN EMPEROR!

Some emperors were bold, decisive, intelligent and fair. Others were weak and cruel. What kind of emperor would YOU make? If you ruled your house, what would your commandments be? Write a list of ten policies (political ideas) for the management of your Home Empire.

QUICK FACTS

Some emperors were not very good people. One, called Caligula, had people executed if they looked at his balding head.

THE ARMY

The Romans were very good soldiers. This was because they were well-trained and disciplined. The army was better organised than their enemies' fighting forces. Roman soldiers were known as 'legionaries' because they were grouped into huge sets of up to 6,000 men, known as a legion. In the 1st century CE, there were around 28 Roman legions in the Empire – that's 168,000 soldiers!

QUICK FACTS

The word salary comes from the word 'salarium', which meant salt in Latin. This was the amount of pay given to a soldier to buy salt, an expensive necessity.

LIFE IN THE ROMAN ARMY

THE UPSIDES
- Travel the world
- A good education
- A job for life
- Regular pay, plus 'booty' (valuable goods seized following a battle)
- A pension or gift of land on retirement

THE DOWNSIDES
- Harsh punishments
- Dangerous battles
- Tough living conditions
- Women unable to join and no marriage allowed
- Back-breaking physical labour

Each legion consisted of between 5,500 and 6,000 men.

A legate was in charge of the entire legion.

A legion was divided into ten large units called cohorts.

LEGION

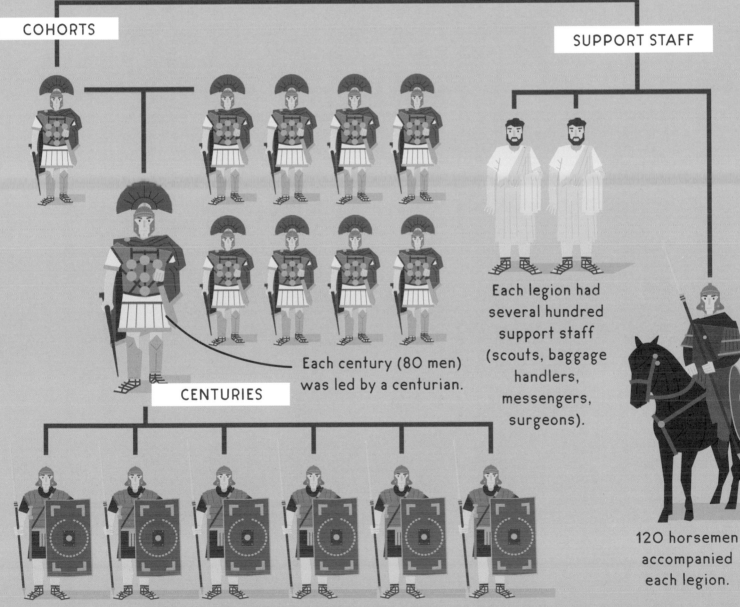

COHORTS

SUPPORT STAFF

Each century (80 men) was led by a centurian.

CENTURIES

Each legion had several hundred support staff (scouts, baggage handlers, messengers, surgeons).

120 horsemen accompanied each legion.

There were six centuries in a cohort, which was made up of 480 men.

WEAPONS AND ARMOUR

Being a soldier gave men a good job and a high status in life – but it was hard work. Legionaries marched up to 30 kilometres a day, carrying heavy equipment and weapons, plus their own personal kit and armour. They carried two javelins, a short sword and small dagger. They also had a shield on their left arm and a helmet, which protected their head.

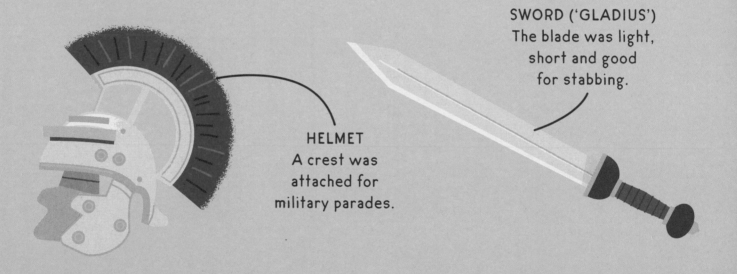

SWORD ('GLADIUS')
The blade was light, short and good for stabbing.

HELMET
A crest was attached for military parades.

MAKE A SHIELD

You need:

A large sheet of corrugated cardboard

Colouring pens

Coloured paper

Scissors

Sticky tape

An adult helper

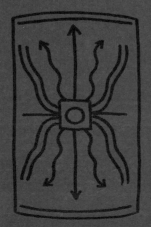

1. Cut out a large rectangle from the cardboard, making sure the corrugations run from top to bottom.
2. Create your design using pens or strips of coloured paper.
3. Attach two small strips of card to make a handle on the other side, bending the shield as you go to create a curved shape.

Legionaries were paid well and expected to contribute money for their uniform and equipment.

JAVELIN ('PILUM')
Soldiers carried two spears to throw at the enemy.

SHIELD ('SCUTUM')
Missiles bounced off its curved sides.

DAGGER ('PUGIO')
This small sidearm was worn on the left side.

BATTLE TACTICS

Legions used powerful weapons on the battlefield, and built siege engines to force their way into enemy cities and forts. Since the wars could last for years, the engines had to be built to last. Some of these machines were flat-packed like furniture, so that they could be wheeled to the battle on carts and then put together. Others had to be built on site.

Hand-to-hand fighting was brutal. The 'testudo' formation looked like a tortoise shell, and gave legionaries some protection.

The onager was a giant catapult that fired rocks or burning tar. Missiles from the onager could hit a target 300 metres away.

Tall siege towers on wheels were rolled up to enemy walls, so that soldiers could fire over the walls into the city.

BUILD A MINI ONAGER

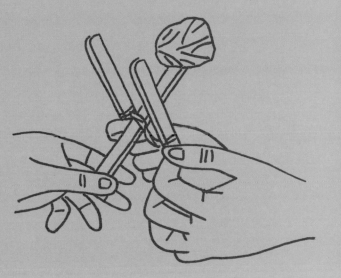

You need:

3 lolly sticks

An elastic band

Paper

An adult helper

1. Get your helper to hold two lolly sticks, one in each hand, and stretch an elastic band between them.

2. Poke the third lolly stick between the stretched loop of the band, then turn it around until you can feel the tension build up.

3. Place a scrunched-up paper missile at the end of your lolly stick 'launcher'... then release!

QUICK FACTS

The Romans also used the powerful ballista, which was like a wind-up crossbow. It fired stones and spears at enemy walls.

WAR AND CONQUEST

The Romans had to fight many battles to remain powerful in the ancient world, and they made many enemies. Along the borders of the Empire, they built huge forts to defend their lands. One great enemy of the Romans were the Carthaginians from northern Africa. The Carthaginian leader Hannibal attempted to attack Rome by crossing the Alps.

Hannibal wanted to surprise the Romans by attacking them by land instead of sea.

Hannibal started out with around 30 to 40 elephants, but lost most of them on the journey, together with around three-quarters of his men.

DESIGN A FORT

Hannibal's route took him from Spain into Gaul (modern-day France) and south into Italy.

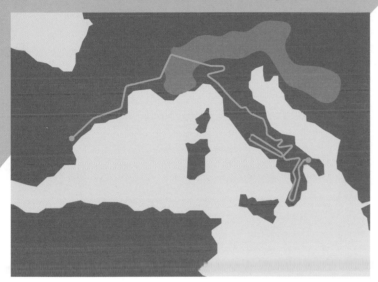

■ The Alps
● Rome

You need:
Plain or graph paper
Pen and pencils
A ruler

Draw a plan for your own fortress town. Think about how you're going to defend it (walls, towers, ditches) and how people will get in and out. How will you lay out the buildings and supplies for the hundreds of soldiers and other people who will live there? Don't forget sleeping quarters, food stores, toilets and stables for the horses. What sort of people will you need to build your mini town?

Once in Italy, Hannibal defeated the Romans in several battles, but never managed to conquer Rome.

QUICK FACTS

Another enemy of Rome were the Huns. They lived in what is now Hungary and Germany. The king of the Huns was called Attila. He gathered together many of Rome's enemies to fight four massive battles against them.

ENGINEERING

The ancient Romans were brilliant engineers. They built grand buildings and a network of roads all over the Empire. Their amazing innovations included arches, aqueducts (to take water to the cities), concrete and even the first central heating system.

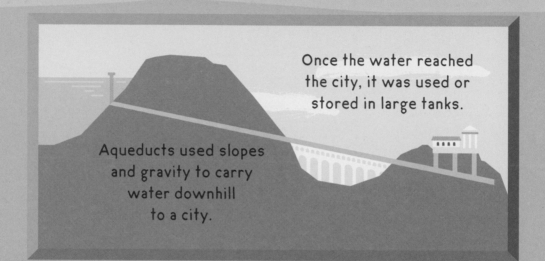

Once the water reached the city, it was used or stored in large tanks.

Aqueducts used slopes and gravity to carry water downhill to a city.

BUILD A BRIDGE

You need:

Toilet roll tubes

Cardboard

Scissors

Sticky tape

An adult helper

1. Cut each toilet roll tube in half lengthways, to make two arch shapes. Use as many tubes as you like.
2. Attach the ends of the halved tubes together using sticky tape, to create one long arch shape.
3. Cut a long strip of cardboard to cover the entire length of the top of your toilet roll bridge.
4. Tape the cardboard strip along the length of the top of the arch.
5. Now, test the strength of your bridge. Start with lighter objects and then try heavier ones... until your bridge eventually collapses!

Roads were made as straight as possible so that people and goods could travel with ease.

The top layers of the road were curved to allow the rainwater to run off to the sides.

Side ditches or stone channels were made, to carry the rainwater away from the roads.

First, the legionaries dug a ditch.

Then they added layers of sand, rubble and stone.

QUICK FACTS

Public toilets were called 'fornicae'. They could fit up to 20 people on two long benches with holes cut out of them at the top. There was no privacy — they were seen as a place to chat and catch up with gossip!

HOMES

Just like today, some houses were very grand, while others were poorly and cheaply built. In the cities, poorer citizens lived with their families in 'insulae'. These were crowded apartment blocks, usually built on top of shops. Wealthier people lived in grand townhouses. These had a central area called an 'atrium', which was a paved courtyard. Rainwater fell through an opening into a central pool, which kept the air cool in the house.

QUICK FACTS

When the volcano Mount Vesuvius erupted in 79 CE, it spewed out lava and ash that buried the town of Pompeii for nearly 1,500 years. When it was uncovered in 1748, the city and many of its inhabitants were found perfectly preserved — the volcanic ash that coated everything had hardened, shielding bodies and houses from decay.

WHICH HOUSE?

Imagine that you are a citizen of ancient Rome. Would you live in a lavish townhouse, with staff to serve you? Or would you live in a cramped insulae along with the rest of your family? What would it be like to live in a home without running water? Do you think a house heated by a hypocaust would feel as warm as a house heated by electricity? Write a description of your imaginary Roman home and what it would be like to live there.

The family's bedrooms were on the ground or first floor.

The walls, ceilings and floors were richly decorated with mosaics and wall paintings.

The study was called the 'tablinum'.

GRAND TOWNHOUSE

The 'atrium' was the courtyard at the centre of the building.

The dining room was known as the 'triclinium'.

The Romans invented a central heating system called a 'hypocaust'. Warm air, heated by a furnace, moved around the building in spaces underneath the floors and in hollow bricks in the walls.

Slaves worked in the kitchen, cooking over a charcoal stove.

THE CITY

Roman cities had large, elegant buildings and open spaces, as well as crowded, bustling streets, jammed with shops and basic housing for poorer people. The central area of most Roman cities was the forum. This was a space where people could meet to trade, do business or talk about politics. Streets led from the forum to the city walls, which protected the city from invasion.

The grand public buildings of Rome would have columns. There were three main styles.

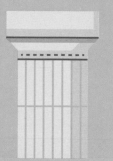

Doric columns were the oldest and simplest style.

The Ionic style is more graceful than the Doric.

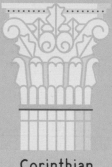

Corinthian columns are the most decorative.

TOWN PLANNING

You need:

Paper

Pens and pencils

A ruler

Think about your own town, village or area, and the location of the main buildings and open spaces — for example, your school, the park, the supermarket or shops, the swimming pool and the cinema. Now draw a plan of how YOU would arrange the main places in your town or area. Where would you like your own home to be? Is there anything you would like to add to the plan?

The centre of most Roman cities was a grand public space called the forum.

Some forums had a platform called the 'rostra', where citizens could stand and give speeches to the crowd. The speakers were called 'orators'.

People gathered at the forum to discuss politics, do business or shop at the markets.

ARTS

The Romans were brilliant artists. They excelled at mixing the art and architecture of other cultures into their own style and producing high-quality artworks, many of which still survive today. The best-known Roman art styles are fresco painting (painting onto walls), sculpture and mosaics (pictures made from small tiles).

Sculptures were carved out of a block of solid marble (a kind of rock), and then painted. Some were made from bronze.

Coloured stones were laid in wet cement to make a mosaic floor.

Fresco painters added colours, in layers, to wet plaster.

CREATE A MOSAIC

You need:

Colourful paper (old magazines, plain or tissue paper, foil)

Large paper or card sheet

Pencil

PVA glue

An adult helper

1. Cut or tear the paper into lots of small pieces.
2. Using your pencil, draw the outline of your face onto the card or paper sheet. Add outlines of your eyes, ears, mouth, nose and hair.
3. Arrange your mosaic pieces on the paper to build up your portrait. When you're happy with the picture, glue the pieces in place.

QUICK FACTS

Statues sometimes had 'removable' heads, in case the person became unpopular. The sculpted head of a new person could then be added in its place!

SOCIETY

In the Roman Empire, you could either be 'free' or a slave. If you were free, you were either a Roman citizen or a 'non-citizen'. Citizens had more rights and didn't have to pay as many taxes to the government. They were also allowed to wear a toga – a long, woollen garment that was wrapped and folded around the body. Citizens were also divided into different social classes. The emperor and the senators were in the top class. Senators had the power to command legions and run parts of the Empire. They could also be priests. Next came the equestrians (knights). Then there were the 'common' orders, including the people who worked as farmers, traders and legionaries. You could tell which class a person belonged to by the way they dressed.

CITIZEN
Wearing a toga was a sign that you were a Roman citizen.

EMPEROR
He was allowed to wear the 'trabea' toga, which was mainly purple.

SENATOR
Important people would wear purple clothes.

SLAVE
Men wore a short
tunic in a coarse,
dark material.

EQUESTRIAN
Knights wore tunics
with narrow,
crimson stripes.

ROMAN WOMEN

In Roman life, women did not enjoy the same rights as men. Very few girls received an education, and women were not allowed to be emperors, to serve in the Senate or the army, or to work in government. Unless they had a very high status, they normally had domestic duties (in the home) and remained under the power of their father, even after marriage. However, women were allowed to inherit their parents' property, which meant that some of them were able to own property and start their own businesses.

QUICK FACTS

Slaves worked in many places, including farms and mines. Those with the best life were the household slaves. They could build a good relationship with their masters. At the end of years of service, some slaves were set free.

Wealthy women's clothes were dyed in bright colours.

CHILDHOOD

Children respected their elders and were obedient to the father of the family. The male children of the rich were taught by tutors or in schools, but also had more time to play. Poorer children were often apprenticed to a trade. A child born into the slave class would follow in the footsteps of his or her parents, often learning how to perform the same skills and trades, or working for the same masters. From the age of ten years, children of ordinary citizens were apprenticed — sent to learn a trade such as weaving or tanning (preparing leather) from a skilled master. Some went to street schools with other children.

Pupils practised their writing on wax-covered boards, using a stylus (a metal pen).

Children played games such as marbles.

LEARN SOME LATIN

The 'pedagogus' was a slave who took responsibility for wealthy boys' education.

QUICK FACTS

Children of the upper classes would learn history, maths and literature. First of all, they had to learn how to read and write in Latin. Pupils learnt by repeating things over and over.

AD HOC
'For this purpose'

AD INFINITUM
'On and on forever'

CARPE DIEM!
'Seize the day!'

PER ANNUM
'For each year'

POST SCRIPTUM
(often 'P.S.' on a letter)
'Written later'

QUID PRO QUO
'One thing for another thing'

TEMPUS FUGIT
'Time flies'

VENI, VIDI, VICI
'I came, I saw, I conquered'

VICE VERSA
'The positions reversed'

FEEDING THE EMPIRE

Rome's main crop was wheat, which was ground to make flour for bread. Much of Rome's grain supply came from Egypt and northern Africa. It would come into the country at Ostia, the port of Rome. Two other major crops were olives and grapes. Olives were squeezed in presses to make oil. Olive oil wasn't only used for cooking, but also in lamps and for washing. Grapes to make wine were also pressed – sometimes by human feet, other times by a machine.

QUICK FACTS

Upper-class Romans often owned a country house and farm. Some of the country estates were very large and specialized in producing certain foodstuffs for the cities.

STARVING ROME

When the Visigoths (an enemy tribe) attacked Rome in 408 CE, they occupied the harbour at the mouth of the River Tiber, so that the deliveries of grain from overseas could not get through. Shortly after the siege began, the daily ration of bread (which was given to each citizen) was halved. Then it was cut to a third. As the weeks went by, people began to starve. The siege worked: after a few months the Senate paid the Visigoths to leave Rome in peace.

Rome needed a reliable supply of food, and plenty of it. When supplies dried up, the angry population rioted!

As well as shipping in food, Rome grew its own crops, including grapes, olives, onions and apples.

Supplies were transported up the River Tiber from the port of Ostia.

RIVER TIBER

OSTIA

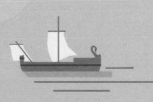

The Roman Empire was dependent on northern Africa for its wheat harvest.

Ships stacked with wheat, olives and wine criss-crossed the Mediterranean Sea from all parts of the Empire.

FOOD AND DRINK

The Romans are famous for their rich diet and lavish meals. In fact, most people ate very simple food and could only dream of the treats served at feasts! Since it was difficult to store fresh food (there were no refrigerators), the Romans developed many ways of preserving food, such as smoking, salting and pickling. If all else failed, they disguised their none-too-fresh ingredients in a salty fish sauce called 'garum'.

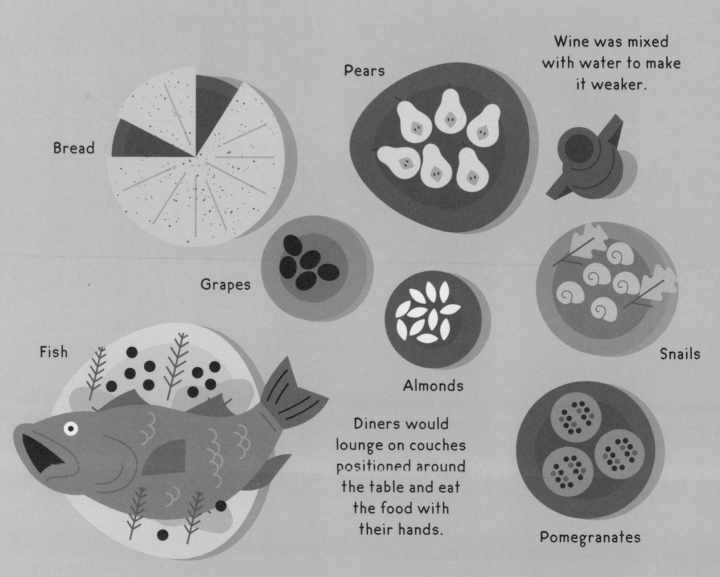

Bread

Pears

Wine was mixed with water to make it weaker.

Grapes

Almonds

Snails

Fish

Diners would lounge on couches positioned around the table and eat the food with their hands.

Pomegranates

A banquet would have included all of the finest foods and wines from around the Empire.

Olive oil

Olives

QUICK FACTS

On city streets, fast-food bars were owned and run by freed slaves. These sold stews and porridge, and wine. The bars were popular among poorer people, who didn't have kitchens and running water in their apartments.

UNUSUAL DISHES

Rich Romans liked their food to be experimental. Their slaves served up plates of animal tongues, while the cooks baked dormice or roasted ostriches, peacocks and the legs of giraffes. One of the more ambitious roasts involved stuffing a chicken inside a duck, the duck inside a goose, and the goose inside a pig — before cooking up the whole lot inside a cow. If the master of the house needed a cold, refreshing drink, he might even send his slaves into the hills to fetch snow for making a flavoured 'slushy'.

TO THE BATHS!

Visiting the public baths was a great way to stay happy and healthy. Male and female bathers visited at different times and some of the larger bathhouses had separate areas for men and women. Bathing lasted several hours. Usually, a bather would do some exercise in the 'palaestra' (an outside gym) before a slave gave him or her a massage with perfumed oils. The slave might also clean the bather's skin by coating it with oil, which was then scraped off using a curved blade called a 'strigil'.

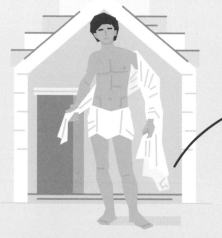

Start off in the dressing room and get changed into a 'subligaculum' (cloth shorts).

Go for a jog, do some stretching or lift some weights in the gym yard.

HEALTHY ROMANS

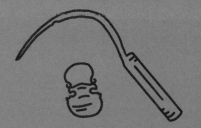

We know about Roman medicines and health treatments from Romans who were writing at the time. Unwashed wool was coated in honey and rubbed into cold sores, or dipped in wine or vinegar to treat a wound. Roman doctors also made medicinal pills using ingredients they could gather from the Mediterranean region. These included onions, carrots, parsley, cabbages, alfalfa, hawthorn, hibiscus and chestnuts.

Have a relaxing massage.

Enter the saunas (sweat rooms) or go into the 'tepidarium', a very warm room.

Now freshen up in the 'frigidarium'. Use the splash basins to have a wash.

QUICK FACTS

After the main bathing experience, the rest of the visit was spent at snack bars, walking in the gardens, listening to a poet, watching an acrobat or playing dice games with pals.

ENTERTAINMENT

Most of Rome's citizens were poor, so the emperor made sure that every person got a monthly ration of grain and free entertainment. People went to see comedies, pantomimes and tragedies, or to hear poets recite their poems. But the most popular entertainment was watching fights between gladiators. There were even fights between people and animals, like lions and bears. Many contests ended in death.

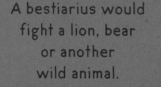

A bestiarius would fight a lion, bear or another wild animal.

CIRCUS MAXIMUS

The Circus Maximus, in Rome, was a vast racing track where up to 255,000 sports fans could watch teams of famous charioteers racing against each other.

Different types of gladiators, often from different countries, fought each other to entertain huge crowds.

A hoplomachus was matched with a murmillo. The murmillo had a larger shield, and a sword rather than a spear.

The secutor was specially trained for fights against the 'net man', retiarius.

QUICK FACTS

Some gladiator fights involved prisoners of war and slaves, who would be made to fight to the death. If neither fighter won, the emperor would ask the crowd to decide who should be killed and who let go.

ROMAN BELIEFS

As the Roman Empire grew, it borrowed beliefs, traditions, and gods from places they had conquered. By 146 BCE, part of Greece came under Roman control, and the gods and goddesses of the Greek religion became part of the Roman religion. Specific temples were dedicated to the worship of each god. There were 12 main gods and goddesses and hundreds of minor ones.

JUPITER:
Lord of the sky

APOLLO:
God of
the Sun

JUNO:
Protector of
marriage

DIANA:
Goddess
of the
wild

VULCAN:
God of fire
and the
forge

CERES:
Goddess of
corn and
harvests

MERCURY:
God of merchants, trade and travellers

VENUS:
Goddess of love and beauty

MINERVA:
Goddess of the city

VESTA:
Goddess of the home and family

MARS:
God of war

NEPTUNE:
God of the sea

SWAPPING PLACES

One festival was called the Saturnalia. Held from 17 to 23 December, it was dedicated to Saturn, the god of seed-sowing and agriculture. During this festival, a household master would swap places with his slave for a few days! Imagine you could swap places with anyone you wanted for a day. Who would it be, and what would you do?

QUICK FACTS

The Romans had gods for almost everything, including Janus, the god of doorways, and Cardea, the goddess of door hinges!

CHRISTIANITY COMES TO THE EMPIRE

The first Christian emperor was Constantine, who converted in around 312 CE. The Christian religion had spread from the Roman province of Palestine. Christians followed the teachings of Jesus of Nazareth, and believed there was only one true god. The Roman authorities thought this rejection of their gods was very suspicious. Constantine is said to have had a vison the night before a battle in which Jesus told him to fight under the sign of the Christian cross. He won the battle and decided to convert to Christianity. Over the next 200 years, more and more Romans converted to Christianity.

CONSTANTINOPLE

Emperor Constantine decided to move the capital of Rome to the Eastern Empire. He built a city called Constantinople (named after himself) on the old city of Byzantium (in modern-day Turkey). Later, another emperor called Heraclius changed the name back to Byzantium. A great church was built there, called Hagia Sophia. You can still visit it in Istanbul, Turkey, today!

The night before a battle, Constantine supposedly dreamt that a cross appeared in the sky, and heard the words 'Under this sign you will win'.

Constantine painted the sign of the Christian cross on his men's shields and won the battle.

Constantine put an end to the mistreatment of Christians and, eventually, Christianity became the official religion of the Empire.

THE END OF THE EMPIRE

The Roman Empire reached the height of its power in the 2nd century CE. But 100 years later, it was in big trouble. It was surrounded by enemies, and it was so big, it was difficult to control. In the 4th century, the Empire split into the Eastern and Western Empires. The Western Empire was under increasingly strong attacks by tribes from northern Europe. Eventually, in 476 CE, Emperor Romulus Augustulus was overthrown and the Western Empire was no more.

QUICK FACTS

The Eastern Empire lasted for another 1,000 years after the fall of the Western Empire. Attacks from the Ottoman Turks eventually brought it to an end in 1453.

THE ROMAN LEGACY

Many Roman inventions and ideas are still around today. The emperor Julius Caesar introduced the 365-day calendar and named the month of July after himself. The Roman alphabet is the most-used alphabet in the world. Roman numbers were used in Europe up until the 1600s, when the numbers we use today took over. Among many other things, the Romans also gave us the idea of trial by jury.

The Roman Empire eventually split into two halves, East and West.

The Western Roman Empire found itself increasingly under attack from 'barbarian' tribes.

The Huns swept west from Asia, threatening the Germanic tribes and Rome.

Visigoths and other Germanic tribes attacked Rome.

WESTERN ROMAN EMPIRE

ROME •

CONSTANTINOPLE •

EASTERN ROMAN EMPIRE

A Germanic tribe called Vandals attacked in northern Africa and Spain.

The Eastern Roman Empire was attacked by the Ottoman Turks, Persians, Avars and Slavs.

GLOSSARY

ARISTOCRATS A member of the upper class of ancient Rome.

BARBARIAN The term 'barbarians' was used by the Romans to describe anybody who wasn't part of the Empire.

CHARIOT A two-wheeled cart pulled by up to four horses, at very fast speeds.

CITIZEN A person in ancient Rome who had certain rights, including the right to elect officials and own property.

CONQUER To defeat or overcome an enemy, usually by using force.

EMPEROR The leader of the Roman Empire. Sometimes, the emperor was even thought of as a god.

EMPIRE The land or lands ruled over by an emperor.

FORT The well-defended living quarters of Roman soldiers, where they lived and trained before going out on a campaign.

MAGISTRATES An official who was chosen by the citizens of Rome to serve the Roman government. When Rome was a republic, the Senate gave advice to the magistrates, who discussed it and decided whether or not to act on it.

MOSAIC Pictures made from small tiles.

SENATE A governing body made up of important or wealthy people in Roman society. The Senate decided on new laws and advised elected officials.

SENATORS A member of the Senate.

SETTLEMENTS A place where people build an area in which to live.

SIEGE When an enemy is surrounded to ensure that no supplies reach the people trapped within.

REPUBLIC A form of government that allowed the people to elect officials, rather than be governed by a king.